poems to make your friends Scream

D1392356

Other books by Susie Gibbs:

Poems to Freak Out Your Teachers
Poems to Annoy Your Parents
Poems to Make Your Friends Laugh

poems to make your friends scream

chosen by Susie Gibbs
illustrated by Jess Mikhail

OXFORD
UNIVERSITY PRESS

OXFORD
UNIVERSITY PRESS
Great Clarendon Street, Oxford OX2 6DP

Oxford University Press is a department of the University of Oxford.
It furthers the University's objective of excellence in research, scholarship,
and education by publishing worldwide in
Oxford New York
Auckland Bangkok Buenos Aires Cape Town Chennai
Dar es Salaam Delhi Hong Kong Istanbul Karachi Kolkata
Kuala Lumpur Madrid Melbourne Mexico City Mumbai Nairobi
São Paulo Shanghai Taipei Tokyo Toronto

Illustrations by Jess Mikhail 2003
Designed by You Know Who

First published 2003

British Library Cataloguing in Publication Data available

ISBN 0-19-276293 1

3 5 7 9 10 8 6 4

Typeset by Mary Tudge (Typesetting Services)

Printed in Great Britain
by Cox & Wyman Ltd, Reading, Berkshire

Contents

Hungry

From the dark primeval depths
of the lake that workmen dredge,

something slippery slithers
to the surface, to the edge,

some strange freak of evolution
oozing over the reeds and sedge.

Something sluggish slides tonight
smoothly through the moonless hedge.

Something sticky, thick and viscous
sludges past the blooms and veg.

Something slimy's slowly climbing
onto the open window-ledge . . .

Nick Toczek

The Bogeyman

In the desolate depths of a perilous place
the bogeyman lurks, with a snarl on his face.
Never dare, never dare to approach his dark lair
for he's waiting . . . just waiting . . . to get you.

He skulks in the shadows, relentless and wild
in his search for a tender, delectable child.
With his steely sharp claws and his slavering jaws
oh he's waiting . . . just waiting . . . to get you.

Many have entered his dreary domain
but not even one has been heard from again.
They no doubt made a feast for the butchering beast
and he's waiting . . . just waiting . . . to get you.

In that sulphurous, sunless, and sinister place
he'll crumple your bones in his bogey embrace.
Never never go near if you hold your life dear,
for oh! . . . what he'll do . . . when he gets you!

Jack Prelutsky

The weirdest Exhibit

The museum galleries
go on for miles,
you see furniture and furnishings,
tapestries and tiles.
You see kitchens where fire grates
are blackened with soot,
but the weirdest exhibit
is a mummified foot.

It's gruesome and gross
but you'll love it the most,
the Egyptian mummified foot.

You can see right inside
where the skin has been ripped,
then you'll notice the bone
and the way it's been chipped.
And beneath the bandage
you see actual flesh . . .
I bet it smelt cheesy
even when it was fresh!

It's gruesome and gross
but you'll love it the most,
the Egyptian mummified foot.

And you open your eyes
And the sun is out
And you jump out of bed
And you sing and shout:
'It was only a dream!'
And you dance around the room
And your heart is as light
As a helium balloon
And your mum rushes in
And says: 'Hold on a sec . . .

What are those two little
Holes in your neck?'

Colin McNaughton

you're new here, aren't you?

I'd better warn you—try not to go at all,
or take a friend. It's not just that there are no locks
and the bigger girls keep barging in, it's . . . well . . .
the one right by the door may be all right
but there's always something inside it,
grunting loudly. The second cubicle
has the octopus—or giant squid—no one's seen
more than its tentacles; but don't worry
it can't get you while you're sitting down—
just watch out when you get up to wipe
and go out backwards. The third one's covered
in scribbled stories that would make
a sewer rat sick. And judging by the mess
some of them have been. The fourth, the furthest in,
is full of spiders, fat black beasts
that drop into your hair. None of them
has any paper except the smelly mass blocking the bowl;
and don't try to wash your hands, the soap
stinks and simply writhes with maggots, and
worms sometimes dribble from the taps. Now,
let me tell you about the Boys' . . .

Dave Calder

My Neighbour Mr Normanton

My neighbour Mr Normanton
Who lives at ninety-five
'S as typical an Englishman
As any one alive.

He wears pinstripes and bowler hat.
His accent is sublime.
He keeps a British bulldog
And British Summer Time.

His shoes are always glassy black
(He never wears the brown);
His brolly's rolled slim as a stick
When he goes up to town.

He much prefers a game of darts
To mah-jong or to chess.
He fancies Chelsea for the Cup
And dotes on G. & S.

Roast beef and Yorkshire pudding are
What he most likes to eat.
His drinks are tea and British beer
And sometimes whisky (neat).

And in his British garden
Upon St George's Day
He hoists a British Union Jack
And shouts, 'Hip, hip, hooray!'

But tell me, Mr Normanton,
That evening after dark,
Who were those foreign gentlemen
You met in Churchill Park?

You spoke a funny language
I couldn't understand;
And wasn't that some microfilm
You'd hidden in your hand?

And then that note I saw you post
Inside a hollow tree!
When I jumped out you turned about
As quick as quick could be.

Why did you use a hearing-aid
While strolling in the park
And talking to that worried-looking
Admiralty clerk?

The day you took the cypher-book
From underneath a stone,
I'm certain, Mr Normanton,
You thought you were alone.

Your powerful transmitter!
The stations that you call!
I love to watch you through the crack
That's in my bedroom wall.

Oh, thank you, Mr Normanton,
For asking me to tea.
It's really all quite riveting
To clever chaps like me.

What? Will I come and work for you?
Now please don't mention pay.
What super luck I left a note
To say I'd run away!

Is that a gun that's in your hand?
And look! A lethal pill!
And that's a real commando-knife?
I say, this is a thrill!

Of course I've never said a word
About the things you do.
Let's keep it all a secret
Between just me and . . .

Charles Causley

Since that thunderstorm . . .

Things have been behaving oddly
Ever since that thunderstorm.
It started when the bath plug
Turned transparent, rose
Like a jellyfish in the water
Tendrils tickling at my toes.
Then there was the telephone
Nibbling my ear, murmuring
'Oh, please . . . Don't put me down.'
The computer mouse began to twitch
Grew furry in my hand. Ran
Up my arm and disappeared.
I've itched all over ever since.
I tell you, I'm scared. I don't dare
Wear my personal stereo headset.

Well, would you? Just wait.
It hasn't reached you—yet.

Trevor Millum

Flesh Creeper

When the moon is the merest sliver,
And thousands of stars stab the sky,
When Grandfather Toad comes crawling,
So do I.

When there's hardly a sound from the river,
And bats begin to fly,
When the Willow Wolf comes prowling,
So do I.

When even the shadows shiver,
And statues start to cry,
When the Old Owl of Merda comes hunting,
So do I.

So do I.

Mike Jubb

The Visitor

A crumbling churchyard, the sea and the moon;
The waves had gouged out grave and bone;
A man was walking, late and alone . . .

He saw a skeleton on the ground;
A ring on a bony hand he found.

He ran home to his wife and gave her the ring.
'Oh, where did you get it?' He said not a thing.

'It's the prettiest ring in the world,' she said,
As it glowed on her finger. They skipped off to bed.

At midnight they woke. In the dark outside—
'Give me my ring!' a chill voice cried.

'What was that, William? What did it say?'
'Don't worry, my dear. It'll soon go away.'

'I'm coming!' A skeleton opened the door.
'Give me my ring!' It was crossing the floor.

'What was that, William? What did it say?'
'Don't worry, my dear. It'll soon go away.'

'I'm reaching you now! I'm climbing the bed.'
The wife pulled the sheet right over her head.

It was torn from her grasp and tossed in the air:
'I'll drag you out of bed by the hair!'

'What was that, William? What did it say?'
'Throw the ring through the window!

THROW IT AWAY!'

She threw it. The skeleton leapt from the sill,
And into the night it clattered downhill,
Fainter . . . and fainter . . . Then all was still.

Ian Serraillier

The Germ

A mighty creature is the germ.
Though smaller than the pachyderm.
His customary dwelling place
Is deep within the human race.
His childish pride he often pleases
By giving people strange diseases.
Do you, my poppet, feel infirm?
You probably contain a germ.

Ogden Nash

Bedbugs' Marching Song

Bedbugs
Have the right
To bite.

Bedbugs
Of the world
Unite.

Don't let
These humans
Sleep too tight.

John Agard

Ghosts

That's right. Sit down and talk to me.
What do you want to talk about?

Ghosts. You were saying that you believe in them.
Yes, they exist, without a doubt.

What, bony white nightmares that rattle and glow?
No, just spirits that come and go.

I've never heard such a load of rubbish.
Never mind, one day you'll know.

What makes you so sure?

I said:
What makes you so sure?

Hey,
Where did you go?

Kit Wright

The Cake That Makes You Scream

Underneath the icing,
Underneath the cream,
Underneath the marzipan
Is the cake that makes you scream.

It's filled with sticky spiders,
Slugs and earwigs too,
And swarms of tiny beetles
Swimming round in glue.

Underneath the icing,
Underneath the cream,
Underneath the marzipan
Is the cake that makes you scream.

It's filled with vampires' fingernails
And all their fingers too,
Crawling from the oozing sludge
Just to tickle you.

> *Underneath the icing,*
> *Underneath the cream,*
> *Underneath the marzipan*
> *Is the cake that makes you scream.*

It's filled with twisted nightmares
Where strawberries turn blue,
And fishes' legs and donkey eggs
Growl and howl and moo.

> *Underneath the icing,*
> *Underneath the cream,*
> *Underneath the marzipan*
> *Is the cake that makes you scream.*

When you cut this curious cake
You don't know what you'll find;
Be careful or the slimy jam
Will climb inside your mind.

But even more important,
Be careful with the knife:
It'll try and slice your tongue out
Before you can take a bite.

Then you won't taste the icing,
And you won't taste the cream,
And the marzipan will slobber out
In a sickening, shapeless scream.

Dave Ward

The Boyhood of Dracula

So we let him join us
In the game of Hide and Seek
Because Joanna said we ought,
She being the biggest of us all
And bossy with it.
And him standing there
All hunched and trembling
In the thin snow by the stable door
Watching us like some poor lost soul
With those great eyes he had.
Well, you'd be a thing of stone
To take no pity on the boy.
You never saw a soul
So pale and woebegone;
His pinched nose raw with cold
And naught to keep the bitter wind
The right side of his bones
But that old bit of musty cloak
He always seems to wear.

Poor little mite
You'd think, to watch,
He'd never played the game before.
Maureen Cantelow,
The parson's youngest girl
From Norton Campion way,
She found him straight away
Hardly bothering to hide at all
Among the meal sacks
In the lower barn.
Poor girl,
She must have cut herself
In there somehow
For as I spied them
Running hand in hand below
She sowed fresh seeds of crimson blood
Across ridged and bitter snow.

Gareth Owen

Mr Watkins Organizes the BCG Injection Queue

Stop talking.
Stop trembling.
One straight line.
Heroes at the front.
Cowards at the back.

There is nothing to worry about.
Nothing.
Apart from the needle.

Forget the stories you've been told
About the pain.
It only hurts about as much as
Being run over.

And besides
Once the first five inches of needle
Have punctured your flesh
Most people
Pass out.

There is very little
Blood. Barely a
Bucketful.

And, of course, it's safe.
Last year we only had
Two fatalities.
So,
Most of you will live
Long enough to do your homework.

John Coldwell

As the witch Said to the Skeleton

WITCH: 'Come on out of that cupboard.'
SKELETON: 'I can't. I haven't got the face to.'

WITCH: 'Oh, come on. There's a dance down the road.
   Why don't you go?'
SKELETON: 'I haven't got any body to go with.'

WITCH: 'Don't you know *anyone*?'
SKELETON: 'No, I haven't got a single ghoul-friend.'

WITCH: 'Well, you needn't sound so sorry for yourself.'
SKELETON: 'Well, I've lost my voice; among other things I
   haven't got a leg to stand on.'

WITCH: 'I suppose you were trying to throw yourself off
   that cliff yesterday?'
SKELETON: 'No, I hadn't got the guts.'

WITCH: 'Scared, eh?'
SKELETON: 'Me scared? You couldn't make *me* jump out of my skin, if you tried.'

WITCH: 'I don't know why I bother with you—you're just a bone-idle old bonehead.'
SKELETON: 'That's right.'

Anon.

Three of a Kind

I stalk the timberland,
I wreck and splinter through,
I smash log cabins,
I wrestle grizzly bears.
At lunch-time if I'm dry
I drain a lake or two,
I send the wolves and wolverines
Howling to their lairs.
I'm Sasquatch,
Bigfoot,
Call me what you like,
But if you're a backpacker
On a forest hike,
Keep a watch behind you,
I'm there, though rarely seen.
I'm Bigfoot,
Sasquatch,
I'm mean, mean, mean.

I pad across the snowfield,
Silent as a thief,
The phantom of the blizzard,
Vanishy, rare.
I haunt the barren glacier
And men in disbelief
Goggle at the footprints
I scatter here and there.
I'm Abominable,
Yeti,
Call me what you choose,
But if you're a mountaineer,
Careful when you snooze,
I'm the restless roaming spirit
Of the Himalayan Range.
I'm Yeti,
Abominable,
I'm strange, strange, strange.

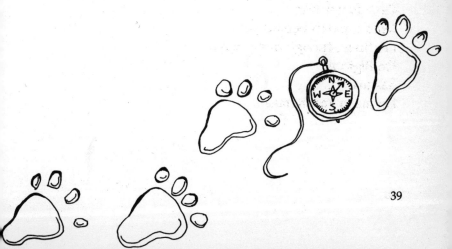

I rear up from the waves,
I thresh, I wallow,
My seven snaky humps
Leave an eerie wake.
I crunch the silly salmon,
Twenty at one swallow,
I tease the silly snoopers—
A fiend? A fish? A fake?
I'm The Monster,
Nessie,
Call me what you please,
But if you're a camper
In the lochside trees,
Before you zip your tent at night
Say your prayers and kneel.
I'm Nessie,
The Monster,
I'm real, real, real.

Richard Edwards

The Skeleton in the Museum

From a glass case,
from a dark room,
from deep inside the museum
the skeleton of a long-dead boy rises.

Listen, his brownish bones clack
as he moves.
Look, his hollow eye sockets
swallow the moonlight.
Watch, his step is certain and sure
as he climbs the hill
to the spot where he was discovered
in a windswept shallow grave.

Brush off the turf and topsoil.
Scrape away the damp, black mud.
Dig out, once again, the uneven bed.
The skeleton of a long-dead Anglo-Saxon boy
lies down again.

Into a cold grave.
Into star light, planet light.
Into Earth's private museum.

John Rice

Pantomime Poem

'HE'S BEHIND YER!'
chorused the children
but the warning came too late.

The monster leaped forward
and fastening its teeth into his neck,
tore off the head.

The body fell to the floor
'MORE' cried the children
'MORE, MORE, MORE

MORE

MORE

Roger McGough

The Friendly Vampire

'Come in,' the friendly vampire said.
'There's room in my tomb for two.
Together we'll have a late-night bite
And I'll share my drink with you!'

The man shook his head.
'I'd rather be dead!'
The vampire gave a grin.
He took a peck
At the poor man's neck
And greedily sucked him in.

John Foster

Miller's End

When we moved to Miller's End,
    Every afternoon at four
A thin shadow of a shade
    Quavered through the garden-door.

Dressed in black from top to toe
    And a veil about her head
To us all it seemed as though
    She came walking from the dead.

With a basket on her arm
    Through the hedge-gap she would pass,
Never a mark that we could spy
    On the flagstones or the grass.

When we told the garden-boy
    How we saw the phantom glide,
With a grin his face was bright
    As the pool he stood beside.

'That's no ghost-walk,' Billy said.
    'Nor a ghost you fear to stop—
Only old Miss Wickerby
    On a short cut to the shop.'

So next day we lay in wait,
   Passed a civil time of day,
Said how pleased we were she came
   Daily down our garden-way.

Suddenly her cheek it paled,
   Turned, as quick, from ice to flame.
'Tell me,' said Miss Wickerby.
   'Who spoke of me, and my name?'

'Bill the garden-boy.'
                  She sighed,
   Said, 'Of course, you could not know
How he drowned—that very pool—
   A frozen winter—long ago.'

Charles Causley

Monster in the Matchbox

There's a monster in this matchbox.
It's a huge green goblin
with teeth like scissors.
Don't make me open it!

There's a monster in this matchbox.
It's only tiny but in the air
it grows and grows until it's the size of a dragon.
Shall I open it?

There's a monster in this matchbox.
It doesn't like little boys or little girls.
It eats them with its sharp scissory teeth.
I'm going to open it!

There's a monster in this matchbox.
It has skin like a rotten cheese
and breath like rotten eggs.
I'm opening it . . . now!

There's a monster in this matchbox
and . . .
Oh dear.
It must have escaped.

Roger Stevens

winter

Winter crept
through the whispering wood,
hushing fir and oak;
crushed each leaf and froze each web—
but never a word he spoke.

Winter prowled
by the shivering sea,
lifting sand and stone;
nipped each limpet silently—
and then moved on.

Winter raced
down the frozen stream,
catching at his breath;
on his lips were icicles,
at his back was death.

Judith Nicholls

Riddle

Voiceless it cries,
Wingless flutters,
Toothless bites,
Mouthless mutters.

J. R. R. Tolkien

Something Scary

Would it be scary
if it was hairy?
What if it wriggled and bit?
Or lay on the ground
all blobby and round,
coated in something like spit?
Sluggish and slimy?
Grim, grey, and grimy?
Would you be frightened of it?

That imp in your head,
the thing that you dread,
what could it possibly be?
Some awful nightmare
that's lurking out there
from which you might never be free.
The thief of your breath
that scares you to death.
Why not reveal it to me?

On a moonlit night
you'd shake at the sight
of spirit or spook or shade.
So you'll be scared stiff
by the merest whiff
of the flesh that clings, decayed,
to my body and head.
I'm alive, though I'm dead.
Now tell me you're not afraid!

Cos I am the beast
that darkness released.
I'm coming towards you, prowling,
with fangs in my jaws
and claws in my paws,
ravenous, roaring, and growling.
If this was a dream
you could wake with a scream
but it's not, so it's no use you howling.

Nick Toczek

RouNd the Park

Where are you going?
Round the park
When are you back?
After dark

Won't you be scared?
What a laugh
A ghost'll get you
Don't be daft

I know where it lives
No you don't
And you'll run away
No I won't

It got me once
It didn't . . . did it?
It's all SLIMY
'Tisn't . . . is it?

Where are you going?
I'm staying at home
Aren't you going to the park?
Not on my own.

Michael Rosen

Nothing Tastes Quite Like a Gerbil

Nothing tastes quite like a gerbil
They're small and tasty to eat—
Morsels of sweet rodent protein
From whiskers to cute little feet!

You can bake them, roast them, or fry them,
They grill nicely and you can have them *en croûte*,
In garlic butter they're simply delicious
You can even serve them with fruit.

So you can keep your beef and your chicken,
Your lamb and your ham on the bone,
I'll have gerbil as my daily diet
And what's more—I can breed them at home!

Tony Langham

Strippers

If you fall in a river that's full of Piranha,
They'll strip off your flesh like you'd skin a banana.
There's no time for screaming, there's no time for groans.
In forty-five seconds you're nothing but bones.

Dick King-Smith

The Vampire

The night is still and sombre,
and in the murky gloom,
arisen from his slumber,
the vampire leaves his tomb.

His eyes are pools of fire,
his skin is icy white,
and blood his one desire
this woebegotten night.

Then through the silent city
he makes his silent way,
prepared to take no pity
upon his hapless prey.

An open window beckons,
he grins a hungry grin,
and pausing not one second
he swiftly climbs within.

And there, beneath her covers,
his victim lies in sleep.
With fangs agleam, he hovers
and with those fangs, bites deep.

The vampire drinks till sated,
he fills his every pore,
and then, his thirst abated,
licks clean the dripping gore.

With powers now replenished,
his thirst no longer burns.
His quest this night is finished,
so to his tomb he turns,

and there awhile in silence
he'll rest beneath the mud
until, with thoughts of violence,
he wakes and utters . . . *blood!*

Jack Prelutsky

The Haunted Launderette

I met a man in a launderette,
With a beard and long white hair,
He was spinning a sheet in a tumble-dryer,
And nobody else was there.

It was cold and dark in that launderette,
There was rain outside in the street,
And never a word did the old man speak,
As he watched his whirling sheet.

When the sheet was dry he took it out,
Then he draped it over his head,
And peering out was his sad, pale face,
But still never a word he said.

'Are you a ghost?' I put to him,
The old man stroked his beard.
'I don't believe in ghosts,' he said,
And promptly disappeared!

Willis Hall

The Dark wood

In the dark, dark wood,
   there was a dark, dark house,
And in that dark, dark house,
   there was a dark, dark room,
And in that dark, dark room,
   there was a dark, dark cupboard,
And in that dark, dark cupboard,
   there was a dark, dark shelf,
And on that dark, dark shelf,
   there was a dark, dark box,
And in that dark, dark box there was a . . .

That Old Haunted House

That old haunted house was so creepy, so crawly, so
   ghastly, so ghostly, so gruesome, so skully-and-bony.
That old haunted house gave me nightmares and
   daymares and shudders and shivers and quivers and
   quavers and quakes.
That old haunted house made my hair stand on end and
   my heart pound-pound-pound and the blood in my
   veins ice-cold-freezing.
That old haunted house gave me goose bumps and
   throat lumps and ch-ch-ch-chattering teeth and the
   sh-sh-sh-shakes.
That old haunted house made me shriek, made me eeek,
   made me faint, made me scared-to-death scared,
   made me all-over sweat.
Would I ever go back to that old haunted house?

You bet.

Judith Viorst

Acknowledgements

We are grateful for permission to reproduce the following poems:

John Agard: 'Bedbugs' Marching Song' from *We Animals Would Like a Word With You* (Red Fox, 1996), copyright © John Agard 1996, reprinted by permission of John Agard c/o Caroline Sheldon Literary Agency.
Charles Causley: 'My Neighbour Mr Normanton' and 'Miller's End' both from *Collected Poems For Children* (Macmillan, 1975), reprinted by permission of David Higham Associates Ltd.
John Coldwell: 'Mr Watkins Organizes the BCG Injection Queue', copyright © John Coldwell 1998, first published in *Dear Future* edited by David Orme (Hodder, 1998), reprinted by permission of the author.
Richard Edwards: 'Three of a Kind' from *The House That Caught a Cold* (Viking, 1991), reprinted by permission of the author.
Mike Jubb: 'Flesh Creeper' from *A Poetry Teacher's Toolkit* (David Fulton, 2002), reprinted by permission of the author.
Dick King-Smith: 'Strippers' from *Jungle Jingles* (Doubleday, 1990), reprinted by permission of Transworld Publishers, a division of The Random House Group Ltd.
Tony Langham: 'Nothing Tastes Quite Like A Gerbil', copyright © Tony Langham 1996, from *Nothing Tastes Quite Like a Gerbil* (Macmillan Publishers, 1996), reprinted by permission of the author.
Roger McGough: 'Pantomime Poem' from *After The Merry Making* (Jonathan Cape, 1971), copyright © Roger McGough 1971, reprinted by permission of PFD on behalf of Roger McGough.
Colin McNaughton: 'Transylvania Dreaming' from *Making Friends With Frankenstein* (Walker Books, 1993), copyright © Colin McNaughton 1993, reprinted by permission of the publisher.
Judith Nicholls: 'Winter' from *Midnight Forest* (Faber & Faber, 1987), copyright © Judith Nicholls 1987, reprinted by permission of the author.
Ogden Nash: 'The Germ' from *Candy is Dandy – The Best of Ogden Nash* selected by Linell Smith and Isabel Eberstadt (Andre Deutsch, 1994), reprinted by permission of Carlton Publishing Group.
Gareth Owen: 'The Boyhood of Dracula' from *Collected Poems for Children* (HarperCollins Publishers, 2000), copyright © Gareth Owen 2000, reprinted by permission of the author, c/o Rogers, Coleridge & White Ltd., 20 Powis Mews, London, W11 1JN.
Jack Prelutsky: 'The Bogeyman' and 'The Vampire', both from *Nightmares, Poems To Trouble Your Sleep* (Greenwillow Books, 1976), reprinted by permission of A & C Black Publishers Ltd.
Michael Rosen: 'Round the Park' from *The Ring of Words* edited by Roger

McGough (Faber, 1998), reprinted by permission of PFD on behalf of
Michael Rosen.

Ian Serraillier: 'The Visitor', copyright © Ian Serraillier 1980, first
published in *A Second Poetry Book* edited by John Foster (Oxford University
Press, 1980), reprinted by permission of Anne Serraillier.

J.R.R. Tolkien: 'Riddle' from *The Hobbit* (Allen & Unwin, 1937), copyright
© J.R.R Tolkien 1937, reprinted by permission of HarperCollins Publishers.

Judith Viorst: 'That Old Haunted House' from *Sad Underwear and Other
Complications* (Atheneum Books for Young Readers, USA., an imprint of
Simon & Schuster Children's Publishing Division, 1995), copyright © Judith
Viorst 1995, reprinted by permission of Lescher & Lescher, Ltd. All rights
reserved.

Dave Ward: 'The Cake That Makes You Scream', from *Nothing Tastes
Quite Like A Gerbil* (Macmillan Publishers, 1996), copyright © Dave Ward
1986, reprinted by permission of the author.

Kit Wright: 'Ghosts' from *Rabbiting On and Other Poems* (Fontana, 1978)
copyright © Kit Wright 1978, reprinted by permission of the author.

**The following poems are published for the first time in this
collection by permission of their authors:**

Dave Calder: 'You're New Here, Aren't You?', copyright © Dave Calder
2003.

John Foster: 'The Friendly Vampire', copyright © John Foster 2003.

Trevor Millum: 'Since That Thunderstorm', copyright © Trevor Millum
2003.

Brian Moses: 'The Weirdest Exhibit', copyright © Brian Moses 2003.

John Rice: 'The Skeleton in the Museum', copyright © John Rice 2003.

Roger Stevens: 'Monster in the Matchbox', copyright © Roger Stevens
2003.

Nick Toczek: 'Hungry' and 'Something Scary' both copyright © Nick
Toczek 2003.

Although we have tried to trace and contact copyright holders before
publication, in some cases this has not been possible. If contacted we will be
pleased to rectify any errors or omission at the earliest opportunity.